THE WORLD'S TOP TEN

MOUNTAIN RANGES

Neil Morris

Illustrated by Vanessa Card

Chrysalis Children's Books

Words in **bold** are explained in the glossary
on pages 30–31.

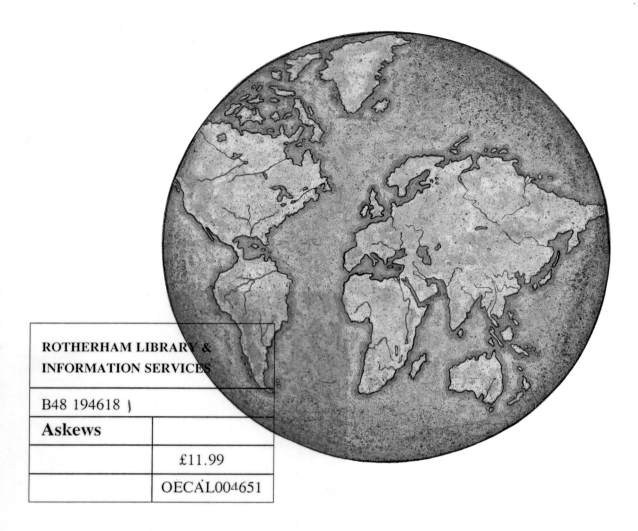

This edition published in 2003 by
Chrysalis Children's Books
The Chrysalis Building, Bramley Road,
London W10 6SP

Copyright in this format © Chrysalis Books PLC
Text copyright © Neil Morris
Illustrations copyright © Vanessa Card

ISBN 1 84138 485 2

British Library Cataloguing in Publication Data for this book
is available from the British Library.

Editor: Maria O'Neill
Designer: Dawn Apperley
Picture Researcher: Diana Morris
Consultant: Elizabeth M Lewis

Printed in China By Imago

Picture acknowledgements:
Robert Harding Picture Library: 10 bottom, 25 top. FLPA: 22
bottom W Wisniewski. Mountain Camera: 5 bottom, 9 bottom,
12 bottom, 28 top all John Cleare, 16 bottom & 17 top Colin
Monteath. NHPA: 15 ANT, 23 top Stephen Krasemann, 26
bottom Karl Switak, 29 bottom. Still Pictures: 8 bottom
Mark Edwards, 18 bottom Bios/Julien Frebet, 20 bottom
Bios/Thierry Thomas, 21 top Bios/Alain Compost, 24 bottom
Foto Nayura/James Philip Nelson, 27 top Bios/Alain Compost.
Tony Stone Images: 5 top Colin Prior. TRIP: 11 bottom, 13
top, 29 top M Jellife, Zefa: 19 top.

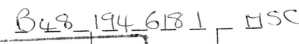

Contents

What is a mountain range?

A mountain range is a group of mountains that lie side by side. Their peaks are separate, but their lower slopes join to form continuous high land. When two or more ranges are linked together, this is called a mountain chain. The longest and highest ranges in the world, such as the Andes, Rockies and Himalayas, are sometimes called mountain systems.

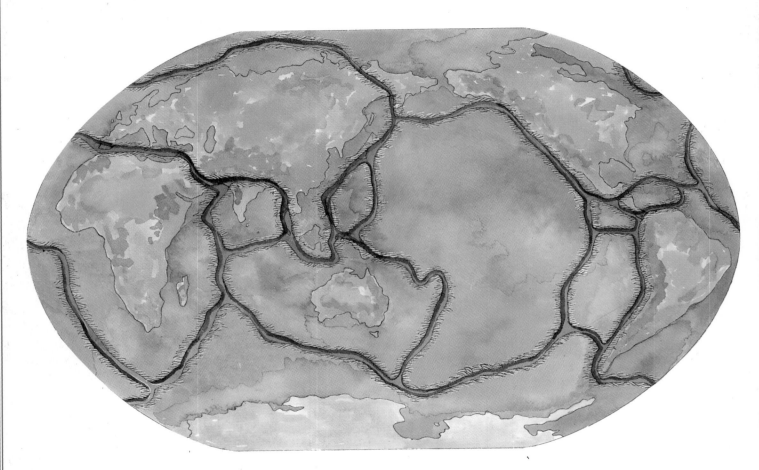

How ranges form

The Earth's surface is made up of an outer layer of rocks, called its **crust**. The crust is cracked into huge pieces that fit together like a giant jigsaw puzzle. These pieces are called **plates.** The plates move against each other, sometimes causing earthquakes, and their edges buckle and crack. Although the plates move only a few centimetres each year, there is enough pressure over millions of years to crumple the rocks into great mountain ranges.

4

New and old ranges

The three longest mountain ranges in the world, the Andes, the Rockies and the Himalayas, lie near plate edges and are still being pushed higher. At the edges of the plates the Earth's crust is weak. Sometimes molten rock from inside the Earth bursts through to form a volcano.

The Great Dividing Range, the Transantarctic Mountains, the Brazilian Coastal Range and the Tien Shan are much older ranges and now lie further from plate edges. They are lower because rain, wind and ice have **eroded** them over millions of years.

The longest mountain ranges

In this book we take a look at the ten longest mountain ranges in the world. We see how similar and how different they are from each other and get to know the people and animals who have made them their home.

The world's highest mountain, Everest, lies among the snow-covered peaks of the Himalayas. This high mountain range is the third longest in the world.

The Dolomites mountain range is part of the Alps, which were formed 40 to 60 million years ago. The mountains have been worn away by the weather into very steep, rocky peaks.

The longest mountain ranges

This map shows the ten longest mountain ranges in the world. The Andes, Rockies, Aleutian and New Guinea ranges are part of the Ring of Fire – a great circle of volcanic mountains around the Pacific Ocean.

Some mountain ranges are on the ocean floor. Their valleys are mainly underwater and their peaks form chains of islands. The Sumatra–Java and Aleutian ranges are like this. One day mountain ranges that are now beneath the ocean may emerge to form new land.

The world's top ten mountain ranges

1	Andes	7200 km
2	Rockies	4800 km
3	Himalayas	3800 km
4	Great Dividing Range	3600 km
5	Transantarctic Mountains	3500 km
6	Brazilian Coastal Range	3000 km
7	Sumatra–Java Range	2900 km
8	Aleutian Range	2600 km
9	Tien Shan	2200 km
10	New Guinea Range	2000 km

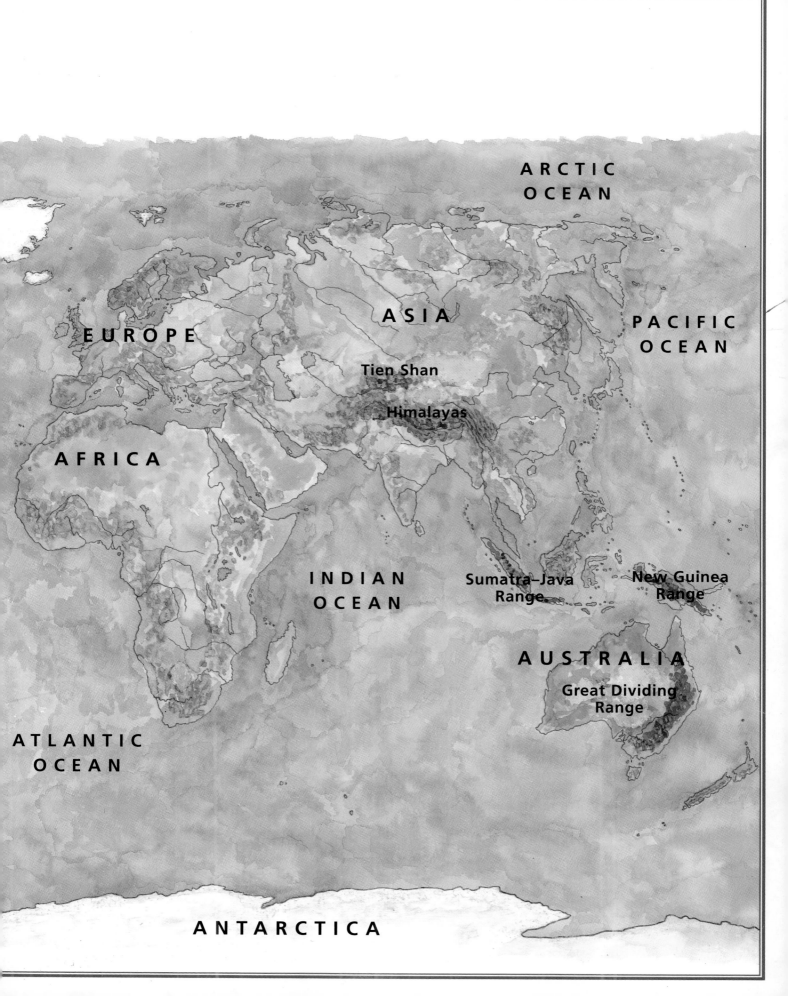

ARCTIC
OCEAN

ASIA

PACIFIC
OCEAN

EUROPE

Tien Shan

Himalayas

AFRICA

INDIAN
OCEAN

Sumatra–Java
Range

New Guinea
Range

AUSTRALIA

Great Dividing
Range

ATLANTIC
OCEAN

ANTARCTICA

Andes

The Andes is the longest mountain system in the world, stretching down the whole of South America. The mountains form part of seven countries – Venezuela, Colombia, Ecuador, Peru, Bolivia, Argentina and Chile.

Contrasting lands

Many mountain ranges make up the Andes. The highest **peak** of all, Aconcagua, is in Argentina. It rises to 6960 metres. There are many kinds of land and land-use in the long Andes region. These include dense forests, **fertile** farmlands and high, empty **plains**. There are big modern cities, and small villages where people have lived the same way for centuries.

La Paz, in Bolivia, is the highest capital city in the world. It lies 3631 metres high in the Andes. More than a million people live there.

VENEZUELA

COLOMBIA

ECUADOR

Maize

PERU

Coffee

Llama

MACHU PICCHU

Spectacled bear

BOLIVIA

LA PAZ

Lake Titicaca

Aymara Indians

PACIFIC OCEAN

CHILE

Condor

Aconcagua

ARGENTINA

Political duck

High lakes

Lake Titicaca lies high in the Andes, between Bolivia and Peru. It is fed by 25 rivers, and is the largest lake in South America. It is also the highest lake in the world, at 3811 metres above sea level. The Aymara Indians live on the shores of the lake. They are farmers and fishermen.

Further south, in Bolivia and Chile, there are many large **salt lakes**. Some are completely dry and white, while others are grey or green. One, called Laguna Colorada, is coloured red by the unusual plants that live in it.

Indian peoples

Before the Spanish **conquest** of South America, the Incas and many other Indian peoples were the main inhabitants of the Andes. When the Spanish arrived in the sixteenth century, they sent their own people to rule the area, and destroyed the Inca empire. In 1911 a well-preserved Inca town called Machu Picchu was discovered high up in the Andes of Peru.

Today Spanish is the official language of all the Andean countries, and many people are *mestizos*, which means people of mixed Indian and Spanish race. Quechua, the language of the Incas, is still spoken by millions of Andean Indians in Bolivia, Ecuador and Peru.

The ruins of the Inca town of Machu Picchu perch on a ridge, 600 metres above the Urubamba River. A royal palace and a temple lie among the ruins.

Rockies

The Rocky Mountains, also called the Rockies, stretch down the western side of North America. This great range is almost 5000 kilometres long, running all the way from north-west Canada to the south-west of the United States. It is the second longest mountain range on Earth, and is part of an even larger system called the Western Cordilleras.

Facts

LENGTH	4800 km
HIGHEST POINT	Mount Elbert, Colorado, USA, 4399m
LOCATION	western North America, Canada and USA

Athabasca Glacier moves slowly down from the Columbia Icefield, high in the Canadian Rockies. Athabasca River flows from the foot of the glacier.

Bighorn sheep

Grizzly bear

CANADA

Moose

Mountain goat

Gold

Vail

Aspen

Skiing

Mount Elbert

USA

Puma

Glaciers and ice fields

The northern end of the Rockies begins in the Yukon Territory of Canada. Further south, the mountains run along the border between the two Canadian provinces of British Columbia and Alberta. Here **glaciers** and rivers of melted ice move down the high valleys. A vast **ice field** surrounds Mount Columbia. Its melting waters feed ice-cold lakes and form rivers that eventually flow into three different oceans – the Arctic, the Pacific and the Atlantic.

National parks

Where the Rockies cross the border between Canada and the United States, there are two famous national parks. Together the Canadian Waterton Lakes and the American Glacier national parks form a large **protected** area known as the International Peace Park. This is the territory of black bears and grizzlies, moose and mule deer, pumas and bighorn sheep. Pumas are also called mountain lions. They have even been found on mountains over 4000 metres high.

Rocky peaks, called the Maroon Bells, tower over Maroon Lake, near Aspen. In winter, when the mountains are covered in snow, this part of the Rockies is very popular for skiing.

Gold and silver

The Rockies are rich in **minerals**. There are large amounts of gold, silver, lead, zinc, copper and **tungsten**. In 1859 there was a great **gold rush** in the Colorado Rockies. Wagons rolled in with signs that read 'Pike's Peak or bust!' At first people did not find much gold, and many wagons rolled eastwards again. This time the signs read 'Busted, by gosh!' But soon gold and silver were discovered, and some people made their fortune. Today the snow-capped Colorado Rockies are more famous for their popular ski resorts, such as Vail and Aspen.

Himalayas

The Himalayas are the world's highest mountain range. They stretch in a wide curve across the border between India and Tibet, through Bhutan and Nepal to northern Pakistan. They continue westwards as the Karakoram Mountains and the Hindu Kush into Afghanistan. This great mountain system is just over half the length of the Andes.

TIBET Nepalese people

Musk deer

Mount Everest

AFGHANISTAN

BHUTAN

NEPAL

Yak

Snow leopard

Lammergeier

Sheep

PAKISTAN

INDIA

Rice

Mountaineer

Climbers walk towards a camp, which is over 6000 metres up Mount Everest.

On top of the world

The ten highest mountains in the world are all in the Himalayas. This includes the highest peak of all, Mount Everest, which lies on the border between Nepal and Tibet. To the people of Tibet, the mountain is known as Qomolongma, or 'goddess mother of the world'.

Mountaineers first tried to climb Everest in 1920, but it was not until 1953 that climbers reached the very top. Recent **satellite surveys** measured Everest at 8863 metres.

FACTS

LENGTH	3800 km
HIGHEST POINT	Mount Everest, Nepal/Tibet, 8863m
LOCATION	southern central Asia

Himalayan kingdoms

In the ancient Indian language of Sanskrit, Himalaya means 'home of snow'. The mountain peaks are all above the **snow line**, which begins at about 4500 metres. This is 1000 metres above the **tree line**.

Two small kingdoms, Nepal and Bhutan, lie in the Himalayas. Both countries have warm, wet lower slopes that can be used for farming. Higher up, the Sherpa people of Nepal and the Drukpa of Bhutan grow rice, barley and other crops. Most people in both kingdoms are Buddhists.

Oxen pull a farmer's plough on the high slopes of Nepal. In the distance are the snowy peaks of Annapurna, the world's tenth highest mountain.

Mountain animals

Some Himalayan mountain people live by herding large shaggy oxen called yaks, as well as sheep and goats. A few yaks still live wild at heights of up to 6000 metres, but so many have been hunted that they have almost died out. The powerful snow leopard hunts wild goats called ibex and small musk deer. The leopard has thick fur to keep warm, but in heavy snow and very cold weather it moves down into the valleys to find food. The Himalayan black bear lives in forests on the lower slopes, sleeping through the cold winter in caves or tree holes.

Great Dividing Range

Australia has only one long range of mountains. The Great Dividing Range stretches all the way from the north to the very south of Australia. Though few of its mountains are higher than 1500 metres, this range is the fourth longest in the world.

Eucalyptus trees

Aboriginal paintings

PACIFIC OCEAN

Coal

Lyrebird

Sheep

Koala

AUSTRALIA

Darling

Blue Mountains

Kookaburra SYDNEY

CANBERRA

Murray

Mount Kosciusko ▲

Snowy Mountains

Snowy River

Dividing the country

The range got its name because it divides the eastern coastal region of Australia from the rest of the country. The distance from the range to the Pacific coast varies from 30 to over 300 kilometres. Europeans settled near the Pacific Ocean, where the land is fertile and the weather is good.

The settlers saw the mountains as a barrier between them and the **outback** and desert areas. At the north end of the range, in Carnarvon National Park, there are **Aboriginal** rock and cave paintings. Aborigines, the original people of Australia, may have lived in these hills 19 000 years ago.

Blue Mountains

The **foothills** of the Blue Mountains begin just 65 kilometres inland from Sydney, Australia's biggest city. The mountains are little more than 1000 metres high, but there are deep valleys and **canyons**, which are very popular with walkers and climbers.

From a distance, the mountains often have a blue haze, giving them their name. This effect is caused by a fine mist of oil given off by the local eucalyptus trees.

FACTS

LENGTH	3600 km
HIGHEST POINT	Mount Kosciusko, 2230m
LOCATION	eastern Australia, across the states of Queensland, New South Wales and Victoria

These sandstone **pinnacles** in the Blue Mountains are called the Three Sisters. Trees cling to the sides of the steep slopes.

The Snowies

In the south of Australia, where it is cooler, some of the Great Dividing Range peaks are snow-capped. There are ski resorts in the Snowy Mountains, not far from the Range's highest peak, Mount Kosciusko. There are several national parks in this area, as well as an important **hydroelectric** scheme. The Snowy River has been dammed, and huge tunnels take water through the mountains to nearby farmland. The water falls hundreds of metres, driving **generators** to make electricity for Canberra, Australia's capital city.

This dam, in Kosciusko National Park, forms part of the Snowy Mountains hydroelectric scheme. It's easy to see why the mountains were given their name.

Transantarctic Mountains

A vast sheet of ice covers Antarctica, the coldest **continent** on Earth. This freezing region surrounds the South Pole and is divided in two by a range of mountains 3500 kilometres long. Antarctica is the world's highest continent, with half its area standing more than 2000 metres above sea level.

Ronne Ice Shelf

Emperor penguins

Blue-eyed shag

Giant petrel

Beardmore Glacier

● SOUTH POLE

▲ Mount Kirkpatrick

ANTARCTICA

Ross Ice Shelf

Icebergs

Whale

ROSS SEA

Adelie penguins

Cold wilderness

Antarctica is very cold and extremely windy. In some areas the average temperature over a whole year is as low as -58°C. Winds can reach up to 320 kilometres an hour, which is three times the speed of a violent storm in other parts of the world. In places the **ice sheet** is almost 5 kilometres thick.

The rocks of some of the taller peaks of the Transantarctic Mountains stand out above the ice. This is unusual, because in most ranges it is the highest peaks that are covered with snow.

Many high regions of the Transantarctic range have rocky peaks and **dry valleys**, such as these in the Prince Albert Mountains.

High mountains overlook a flat layer of thick ice. This ice shelf forms the coast of the Ross Sea.

Glaciers and icebergs

There are many massive glaciers in the Transantarctic Mountains. The longest of them, the Beardmore Glacier, feeds a huge sea of ice at the foot of the mountains. This is called the Ross **Ice Shelf**. Gigantic chunks of ice break off from the edge of the shelf, becoming icebergs that float away to sea.

FACTS

LENGTH	3500 km
HIGHEST POINT	Mount Kirkpatrick, 4528m
LOCATION	Antarctica, from Victoria Land to the Weddell Sea

The mountains, glaciers, cold and wind made the journey to the South Pole a terrible struggle for explorers. In 1911 Robert Scott and four others climbed the Beardmore Glacier to reach the high Antarctic **plateau** and finally the Pole. There they found a Norwegian flag – Roald Amundsen's team had beaten them to it. Scott and his men all died on their way back to base.

Changing climate

Scientists now think that the Earth's climate is becoming warmer. There are many signs of this happening in Antarctica. The two main types of flowering plant are spreading, and glaciers are beginning to move faster and melt more quickly. More icebergs are breaking away from the ice shelf too. The weight of the ice on the land surface presses the land down, so if the ice melts, the land will begin to rise. The Transantarctic Mountains may then become even higher than they are now.

Brazilian Coastal Range

The Brazilian Coastal Range stretches for 3000 kilometres close to the Atlantic coast of Brazil. The highest peak is Pico da Bandeira, which rises to 2890 metres. This mountain is in the south of Brazil, not far from Rio de Janeiro.

Diamonds

BRAZIL

Anteater

Gold

Tupi Indians

Carnival

Pico da Bandeira ▲

RIO DE JANEIRO

Great Escarpment

SAO PAULO

Coral snake

ATLANTIC OCEAN

Armadillo

Ancient rocks

The Coastal Range forms the edge of a plateau that stretches towards the middle of Brazil. In this area there are some of the oldest rocks on Earth. Scientists have discovered that some of them date back to when the Earth was forming, at least 4600 million years ago. Since then, the mountains have been worn away by rain and wind. This process, called **weathering**, has smoothed the mountains so that the landscape is mainly low and rounded.

Coffee plants grow well in the highlands, and there are many large plantations. Brazil is the world's biggest producer of coffee.

Highland barrier

Tupi Indian tribes lived in the forests of eastern Brazil long before Europeans arrived. Then 500 years ago an explorer named Pedro Alvares Cabral claimed Brazil for Portugal. At first the range of highlands formed a barrier for the new settlers. They stayed on the strip of low land that runs along the Atlantic coast. Today, most Brazilians still live between the coast and the mountains. Huge cities have grown up, including São Paolo and Rio de Janeiro. Nearly 17 million people live in São Paolo, the biggest city in South America.

FACTS

LENGTH	3000 km
HIGHEST POINT	Pico da Bandeira, 2890m
LOCATION	eastern Brazil, near the Atlantic coast

Mountain riches

To the north of Rio de Janeiro, a series of mountain blocks rises like steps. South of Rio, the edge of the mountain range is steeper and higher, forming a single barrier like a wall. This steep edge is known as the Great **Escarpment**. When settlers at last made their way across this barrier and into the mountains, they found gold, diamonds and other precious stones. The mountains are still mined for **iron ore**, **manganese** and **quartz**.

Hundreds of years ago, settlers rushed to the Brazilian mountains in search of gold. Today, gold is still mined in the region.

Sumatra–Java Range

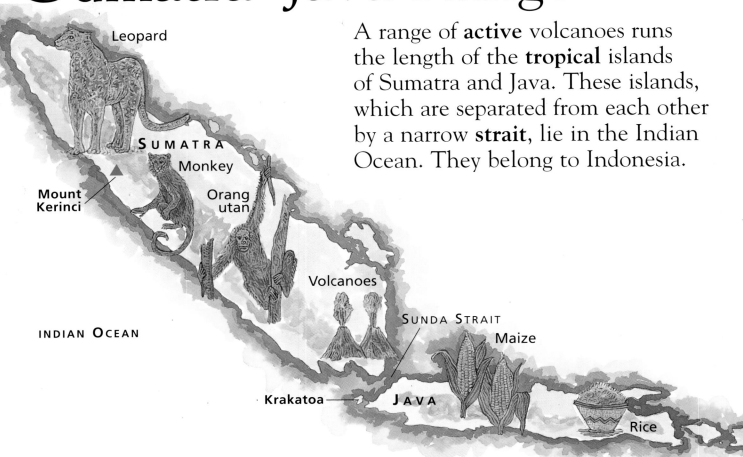

A range of **active** volcanoes runs the length of the **tropical** islands of Sumatra and Java. These islands, which are separated from each other by a narrow **strait**, lie in the Indian Ocean. They belong to Indonesia.

Leopard

SUMATRA

Monkey

Orang utan

Mount Kerinci

Volcanoes

SUNDA STRAIT

Maize

INDIAN OCEAN

Krakatoa

JAVA

Rice

A fisherman's cabin on Lake Kerinci. The lake is in a valley near Mount Kerinci, the range's highest point.

The Sunda Shelf

The islands of Sumatra and Java are really the tops of mountains. They are on the southern edge of the Earth's Eurasian Plate. This region is called the Sunda Shelf. Just south of the islands, where the Sunda Shelf meets the Australian Plate, is the Java Trench. Here the ocean bed plunges to 7725 metres below sea level. The movements of the two plates have created the string of volcanoes that runs along the islands.

Anak Krakatoa throws out a fountain of **lava** as it erupts. This active volcano now forms an island over a kilometre across.

Violent eruption

In 1883 the volcano Krakatoa, in the Sunda Strait, erupted. The explosion destroyed two thirds of the island and was heard 5000 kilometres away. The sea bed moved, causing a series of giant ocean waves called **tsunamis**. When these 40-metre waves hit the shores of Sumatra and Java, villages were destroyed and over 36 000 people were killed. In 1927, a new volcanic island appeared. It is called Anak Krakatoa, or Child of Krakatoa, and it erupts, much less violently, about once a year.

FACTS

LENGTH	2900 km
HIGHEST POINT	Mount Kerinci, Sumatra, 3806m
LOCATION	Sumatra and Java, Indonesia, in the Indian Ocean

Active volcanoes

There are about 500 active volcanoes in the world, and 50 of these are on Java. In recent years there have been at least 17 eruptions on the island. But more people live on Java than on the other Indonesian islands. One reason for this is that the island's volcanic ash is full of good chemicals that enrich the soil. Rice, maize and many other crops grow well in Java's volcanic soil, and these provide food for the large population.

Aleutian Range

The world's eighth longest mountain range stretches out as a **peninsula** and then a string of islands from the north-west tip of North America. The Aleutian Range is part of Alaska, the largest state in the USA. The Aleutian Islands, part of the range, separate the Pacific Ocean from the Bering Sea.

Aleut

Mount Katmai

Puffin

Arctic tern

BERING SEA

Unimak Island

Seal

Fish

PACIFIC OCEAN

Mount Shishaldin

Adak Island

Whale

Alaska Peninsula

A series of mountain ranges forms a huge curve around Alaska's Pacific coast. First there are the Coast Mountains, then the Alaska Range, which is over 1100 kilometres long. Finally the Aleutian Range runs along the Alaska Peninsula. The peninsula's most famous peak is Mount Katmai, a volcano which erupted with terrible force in 1912. The eruption created the Valley of Ten Thousand Smokes, which years later was still giving off steam and volcanic gases.

Today the Valley of Ten Thousand Smokes looks like an empty desert, surrounded by snow-capped volcanoes.

22

An inlet on Adak Island, 1000 kilometres from the tip of the Alaska Peninsula. This remote island rises to a height of 1196 metres.

Foggy islands

The Aleutian Range continues from the tip of the Alaska peninsula as a chain of 150 islands. These are all the tops of volcanic mountains, and their lower slopes are covered by sea. The highest peak, measured from sea level, is on the largest island, Unimak.

The climate on these islands and in their mountains is cool, wet and foggy. The fog is caused when warm air from the Pacific meets cold air coming from the Bering Sea.

Aleut people

The first people to live on the Aleutian Islands were relatives of the Inuit who crossed from the Alaskan mainland about 4000 years ago. The Aleuts depended on the sea for food, hunting whales, seals and sea otters from their **kayaks**. They caught fish with spears and fishhooks. Aleut families lived in homes dug into the ground and covered with grass, animal skins and layers of earth. Today there are only a few thousand Aleuts left. Some run fishing boats and others work in fish **canneries**.

FACTS

LENGTH	2600 km
HIGHEST POINT	Mount Shishaldin, Unimak Island, 2861m
LOCATION	Alaskan Peninsula and Aleutian Islands, between the north-west Pacific Ocean and the Bering Sea

Tien Shan

In central Asia, the Tien Shan range forms a border between Kyrgyzstan and its neighbour, China. Kyrgyzstan belonged to the former Soviet Union and became an independent country in 1991.

Sheep

KYRGYZSTAN

Pik Pobedy

Ibex

● **URUMQI**

CHINA

TAKLA MAKAN DESERT

Kyrgyz People

Snow leopard

Tulips

Far from the sea

At the eastern end of the range, the Tien Shan mountains stretch into Xinjiang, the largest province in China. Its capital, Urumqi, is 2500 kilometres from the coastline. This is further from the sea than anywhere else in the world. Just south of the Tien Shan is the Takla Makan desert. The desert is surrounded by mountains and is so far inland that it hardly ever rains.

There is a story that Tamerlane, a fourteenth-century Mongol chief, told his soldiers to put a stone in a pile as they crossed the Tien Shan. When they came back from battle, each man took back a stone, so Tamerlane knew how many men he had lost.

The Tien Shan peaks can be seen from this green valley in eastern Kyrgyzstan.

Kyrgyz people traditionally keep camels for milk and transport. These people are crossing a plateau near the Tien Shan.

Heavenly mountains

The Tien Shan is a very beautiful area, and in Chinese its name means Heavenly Mountains. There are deep gorges, rushing rivers, **alpine** meadows, glaciers and snow-capped peaks. Ibex and mountain sheep graze on high **pasture**, and are occasionally hunted by the rare snow leopard. Wild fruit trees, roses and tulips grow on many of the lower slopes.

FACTS

LENGTH	2200 km
HIGHEST POINT	Pik Pobedy, Kyrgyzstan, 7439m
LOCATION	central Asia, Kyrgyzstan and Xinjiang province, China

Wandering peoples

The Chinese Uygurs and the native people of Kyrgyzstan both follow the religion of Islam. Their ancestors were **nomads** who ruled a large part of northern China many centuries ago.

Some Kyrgyz people still wander the highland areas, living in felt tents called yurts. But most Uygurs have settled as farmers. They are also famous for their silverwork, and make their own musical instruments to play along to their traditional dances.

New Guinea Range

The tenth longest mountain range runs down the middle of New Guinea. This mountainous island lies in the Pacific Ocean. Its western half, called Irian Jaya, belongs to Indonesia. The eastern half is a separate country called Papua New Guinea.

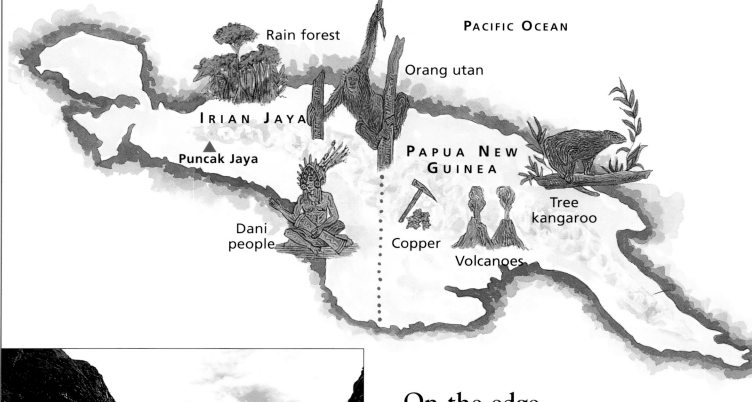

Rain forest

PACIFIC OCEAN

Orang utan

IRIAN JAYA

Puncak Jaya

PAPUA NEW GUINEA

Dani people

Copper

Volcanoes

Tree kangaroo

On the edge

Like all volcanic mountain ranges, the New Guinea range lies at the edge of one of the plates that make up the Earth's crust. New Guinea is at the north end of the Australian Plate, near the boundary where it meets the Pacific Plate. There are few active volcanoes on the island, but in 1951 a glowing cloud of gas, steam and **molten** rock killed 2000 people at the foot of Mount Lamington.

The soil on volcanic mountain ranges is very fertile. In New Guinea, lush forests cover the highlands, and streams rush down the slopes.

Copper City

Puncak Jaya is the highest mountain between the Himalayas and the Andes. At 5030 metres, it is the highest point in the New Guinea Range. The area is difficult to reach, partly because of dense tropical **rain forest** on the lower slopes.

But in 1936 a Dutch scientist discovered copper in the mountains. Bulldozers were flown in to build a road, and by the 1970s a huge mine was producing thousands of tonnes of copper. A whole town grew up around the mine. It was named Tembagapura, or Copper City. The project has caused many problems, including **deforestation** and **pollution**.

Although New Guinea lies just south of the **Equator**, Puncak Jaya and the island's other high mountains are capped with snow and ice all year round.

FACTS

LENGTH	2000 km
HIGHEST POINT	Puncak Jaya, Irian Jaya, Indonesia, 5030m
LOCATION	New Guinea, in the Pacific Ocean

Highland villages

Many different peoples, including the Dani and the Jalé, live in the highlands of New Guinea. Their villages are in remote areas of the mountains, and their traditional way of life remained undisturbed for many years. But in recent times, copper and other metals have been discovered, and there has been an increase in tourism to remote regions of the world. As a result, the lives and homeland of these peoples are changing.

The world's mountain ranges

The five longest ranges in the world are in five different continents – South America, North America, Asia, Australia and Antarctica. There are big ranges in the other two continents, Europe and Africa, too.

Alps

The Alps are the highest range in Europe, although the Scandinavian Range in Norway and Sweden, and the Apennines in Italy are longer. The Alps stretch for just over 1000 kilometres, from south-east France, across Italy, Switzerland, Germany and Austria, to the Hungarian lowlands. Europe's highest mountain, Mont Blanc (see right), lies on the border between France and Italy. It is 4807 metres high and has more than 20 glaciers. Many rivers and streams flow down from the glaciers to the valleys below. A road tunnel runs through Mont Blanc, from France to Italy.

Urals

The northern end of the Urals Range lies above the **Arctic Circle**, in north Russia. The range runs north-south for 2000 kilometres, forming the border between Europe and Asia. The highest peak is Mount Norodnaya, which is 1894 metres high. The Urals are rich in iron, nickel, copper and gold. In the south, cattle graze on the lower slopes. The Ural River flows 2535 kilometres from the mountains to the Caspian Sea.

Atlas

The Atlas Mountains (right) are a mountain chain, made up of different ranges leading into each other. The chain is over 1900 kilometres long. It stretches from the Atlantic coast of Morocco, across northern Algeria to Tunisia and the Mediterranean Sea. In many places, the Atlas Mountains form the northern edge of the Sahara, the largest desert in the world. Despite the heat lower down, many high Atlas mountains are covered with snow for much of the year. This includes the highest peak, Mount Toubkal, which is 4165 metres high.

Appalachians

The wooded hills of the Green Mountains in Vermont, USA, are part of the Appalachians. This great range runs down the east coast for almost 2000 kilometres, from the northern state of Maine to Alabama in the south.

The highest peak is Mount Mitchell, in North Carolina, which is 2037 metres high, but the mountains were much higher when they were formed around 300 million years ago. There are many national parks along the whole range.

Glossary

Aboriginal painting in Australia.

Aboriginal Relating to the Aborigines, the original people of Australia.

active (Of a volcano) that may erupt at any time.

alpine On high mountains.

Arctic Circle An imaginary circle around the Earth near the North Pole.

cannery A factory where food is put in cans.

canyon A deep split in the Earth that forms a high, narrow valley.

conquest Taking control by force.

continent A huge land mass.

crust The Earth's outer shell.

deforestation Clearing land of trees.

dry valley Valley that was formed by water but is now dry.

Equator An imaginary circle around the middle of the Earth.

erode To wear away.

escarpment A steep slope.

fertile Having rich soil.

foothills The lower hills around the edge of a mountain range.

generator A machine that turns one form of energy, such as the power of water, into electricity.

glacier A mass of permanent ice that moves down a mountain very slowly.

gold rush Large numbers of people moving to a region where gold has been found.

hydroelectric Making electricity using the force of moving water.

Aleuts paddling their kayak.

ice field A mass of ice covering a large area of high land in the mountains.

ice sheet A thick layer of ice covering a large area of land.

ice shelf A mass of ice floating on the sea and attached to land.

iron ore A mineral that is mined to produce iron.

kayak A light canoe-like boat covered with animal skins.

lava Molten rock thrown out of a volcano.

manganese A grey-white metal that is used to make steel.

mineral Any natural, solid material found in the earth that does not come from plants or animals.

molten Melted; turned into liquid.

nomads People who wander from place to place to find food and grazing land for their animals.

outback Australian bush country.

pasture Grassy land on which cattle can graze.

peak The pointed top of a mountain.

peninsula A strip of land that juts into the sea; it is almost an island.

pinnacle A thin, upright piece of rock.

plain Flat countryside with few trees.

plate A huge piece of the Earth's crust.

plateau A flat area of high land.

pollution Damage caused by poisonous and harmful substances.

protected Looked after and kept from harm.

Tupi Indians in the Brazilian rain forest.

quartz A mineral used to make glass, and also used as a gemstone.

rain forest Thick forest found in warm tropical areas of heavy rainfall.

salt lake A lake that often dries up in hot weather, leaving a thick layer of salt.

satellite survey Measurements taken by photographing the Earth from space.

snow line The height on a mountain above which there is always snow.

strait A narrow sea channel between two areas of land.

tree line The height on a mountain above which no trees grow.

tropical Found in the tropics, the hottest part of the Earth.

tsunami A giant ocean wave caused by a volcanic eruption.

tungsten A hard, grey metal.

weathering The wearing away of rocks by the weather.

Nomads outside their tent, in central Asia.

31

Index

Words in **bold** appear in the glossary on pages 30-31.